ORIGAMI
for Parties

Games

Place settings

Puppets and planes

Push and pull animals

Kazuo Kobayashi
Makoto Yamaguchi

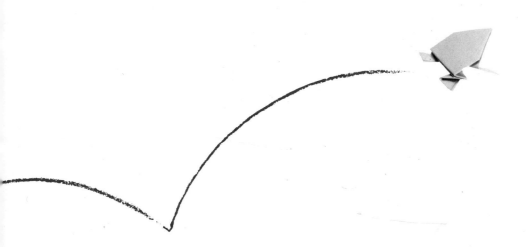

KODANSHA INTERNATIONAL
Tokyo • New York • London

You are invited to a party...

Contents

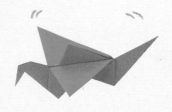

1. Which is the front side of the paper?

Origami paper has one colored and one plain (white) side. Unless instructed otherwise, start with the colored side face down so that it will become the outside of the completed origami. Similarly if you are using paper colored on both sides, the color you wish to appear on the outside should be face down when you begin.

2. What size paper should I use?

The standard 6"×6" size is the most commonly used and most convenient to fold. However, depending on the origami, smaller paper, rectangular paper (notebook paper, standard 8"×11"), or newspaper may be used. Please check the instructions for each origami.

3. Where can I get origami paper?

In the United States, origami paper can be purchased in Japanese goods stores, hobby and craft shops, and select stationery outlets. (In Japan, most stationery stores, department stores, and specialist paper shops stock origami of various colors, patterns, sizes, and quality.) Basically, no special paper is required, and you can use any paper you happen to have at hand, from memo to wrapping paper. Addresses of some origami associations, many with members from around the world, are listed on the inside back cover, and these groups will be able to provide you with further useful information.

Lines	
————————	indicates previous fold(s).
— — — — — — —	indicates folds to be made in that step.
—··——··——··—	indicates that paper should be folded behind, or under.
·················	indicates (1) hidden portion or (2) position after fold.

Symbols	
Fold forward along dotted line.	
Fold under along line.	

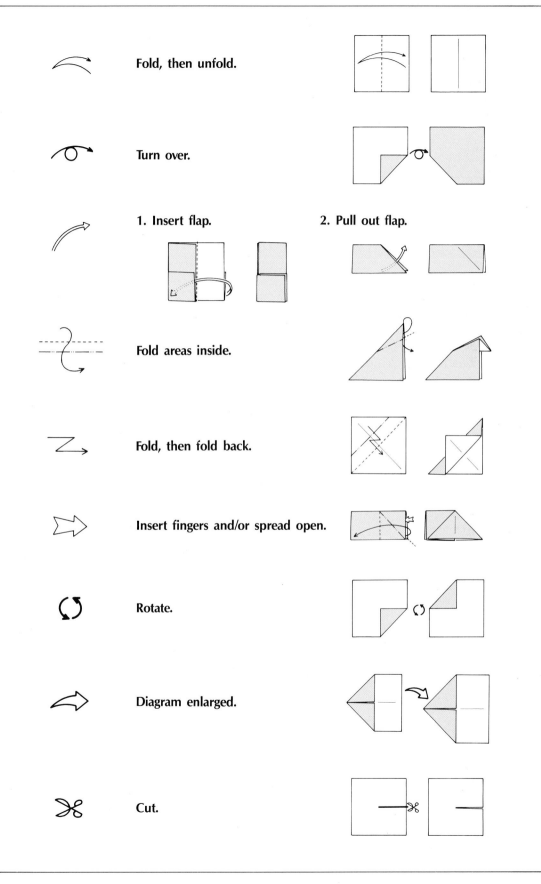

Fold, then unfold.

Turn over.

1. Insert flap.   2. Pull out flap.

Fold areas inside.

Fold, then fold back.

Insert fingers and/or spread open.

Rotate.

Diagram enlarged.

Cut.

SWAN CENTERPIECE

Arrange a small bouquet of flowers in the swan for a pretty table decoration. A small stone or weight will prevent the centerpiece from tipping over. For best results, use an attractive medium-weight paper.

Makoto Yamaguchi

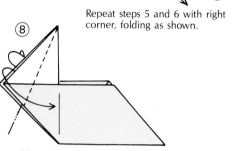

⑨ Repeat steps 5 and 6 with right corner, folding as shown.

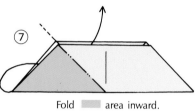

⑧ Fold top layer forward to vertical crease. Repeat on other side.

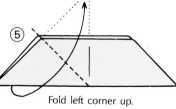

⑦ Fold ▨ area inward.

① Fold paper in half. Unfold.

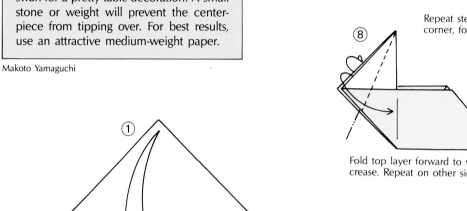

⑥ Unfold.

② Fold in half in opposite direction. Unfold.

③ Fold top and bottom corners in to meet in center.

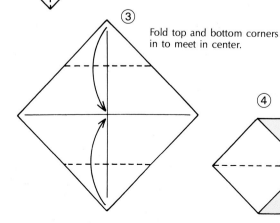

⑤ Fold left corner up.

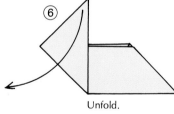

④ Fold in half, bringing bottom edge up to match top edge.

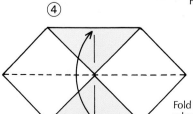

⑩ Fold ▨ area inward (as in step 7).

⑪ Open to form diamond, then flatten.

⑫ Fold corners in to meet at center.

⑬ Fold in half.

⑭ Fold ▨ area back along dotted line, unfold, then fold ▨ area in to form head.

⑮ Push white triangle down to form tail.

⑯ Fold ▨ area under, then unfold. Insert finger at white arrow and open cavity while pushing at black arrow. ▨ area will form triangular base.

FORK AND KNIFE HOLDER

Use paper the same length as the silverware for a perfect fit. The width of the holder can be adjusted in steps 4 and 5.

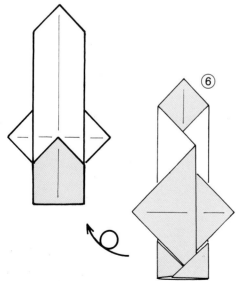

Makoto Yamaguchi

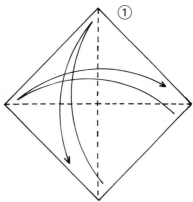

Fold in half in both directions. Unfold.

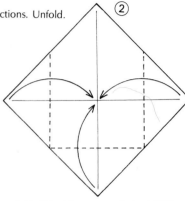

Fold all but top corner in to center.

Origami should look like this. Turn over.

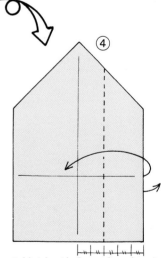

Fold right side forward, so that triangle at back (made in step 2) protrudes.

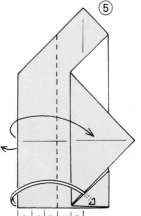

Repeat with left side. Insert bottom corner of left edge into slip at lower right-hand corner.

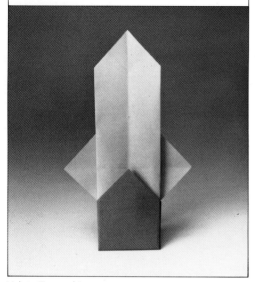

Origami should look like this. Turn over.

PAPER CUP

If you use foil or waterproof paper the cup will last longer. Use a large piece of paper to make a bowl for popcorn or potato chips.

Traditional

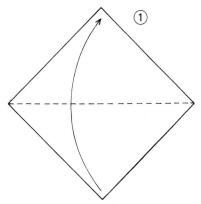

① Fold in half.

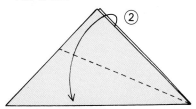

② Fold right edge of top layer down, aligning with bottom edge.

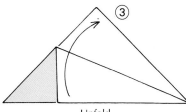

③ Unfold.

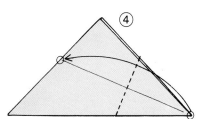

④ Fold to match circled points.

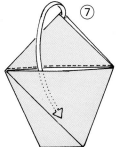

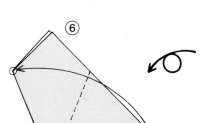

⑥ Fold to match circled points.

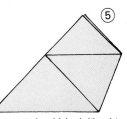

⑤ Origami should look like this. Turn over.

⑦ Fold corner of front layer down and slide it into front flap. Repeat on other side.

NAPKIN RING

Patterned paper will add an extra splash of color. You can make a ring for your finger with a small (3″ x 3″) piece of paper.

Makoto Yamaguchi

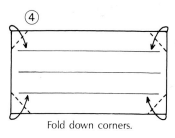

④ Fold down corners.

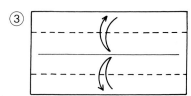

③ Fold bottom and top edges in to center line. Unfold.

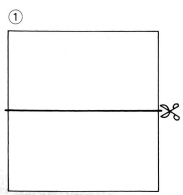

① Cut paper in half.

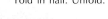

② Fold in half. Unfold.

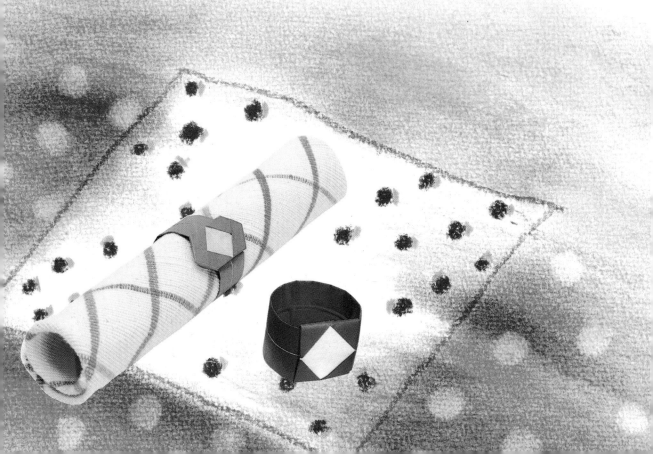

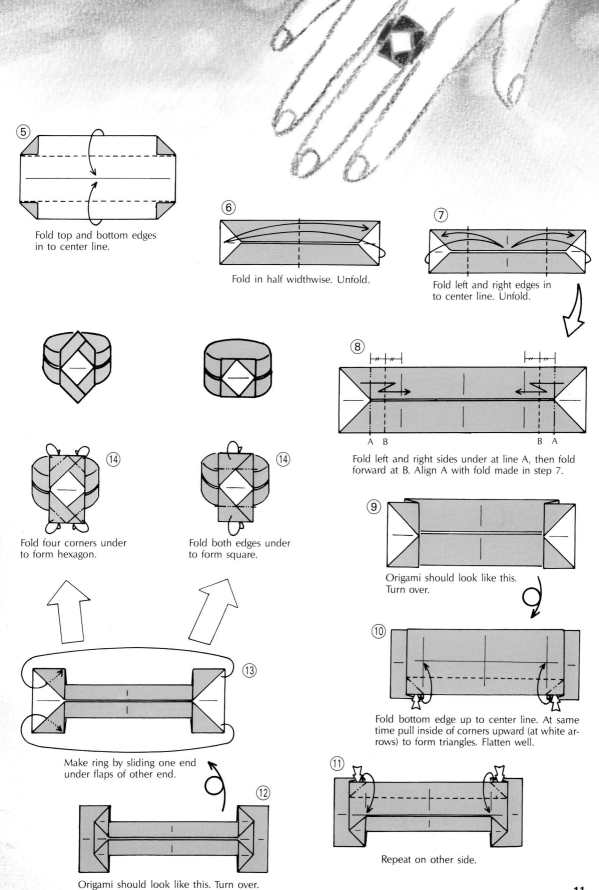

⑤ Fold top and bottom edges in to center line.

⑥ Fold in half widthwise. Unfold.

⑦ Fold left and right edges in to center line. Unfold.

⑧ Fold left and right sides under at line A, then fold forward at B. Align A with fold made in step 7.

A B   B A

Fold four corners under to form hexagon.

⑭ Fold both edges under to form square.

⑨ Origami should look like this. Turn over.

⑩ Fold bottom edge up to center line. At same time pull inside of corners upward (at white arrows) to form triangles. Flatten well.

⑬ Make ring by sliding one end under flaps of other end.

⑪ Repeat on other side.

⑫ Origami should look like this. Turn over.

CANDY DISH

The base of the dish (see step 19) will be one-fourth the length of the paper. Use two sheets, each a different color, for a more striking effect. Fill the dish with candy, pretzels, or other party favorites.

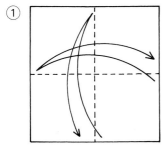

Traditional

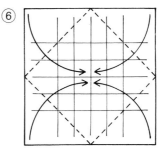

Origami should look like this. Turn over.

Fold four corners in to center.

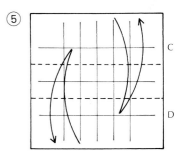

Fold bottom edge to C, then unfold.
Fold top edge to D, then unfold.

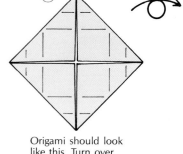

Fold in half in both directions. Unfold.

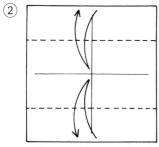

Fold top and bottom edges in to center line. Unfold.

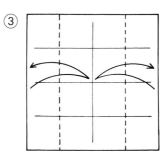

Fold left and right edges in to center line. Unfold.

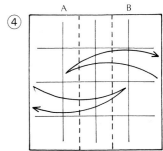

Fold right edge to A, then unfold.
Fold left edge to B, then unfold.

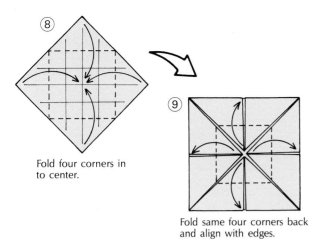

⑧ Fold four corners in to center.

⑨ Fold same four corners back and align with edges.

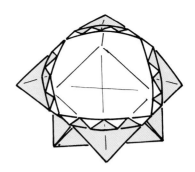

⑩ Origami should look like this. Turn over.

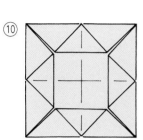

⑪ Fold one square in half as shown.

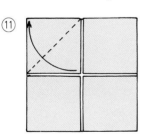

⑫ Fold corner of top layer to edge of triangle.

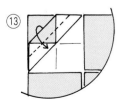

⑬ Fold in half.

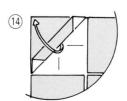

⑭ Unfold to position in step 12.

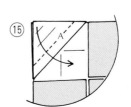

⑮ Fold corner in to center along crease A (made in step 13).

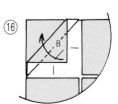

⑯ Fold corner out along crease B (made in step 12).

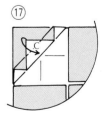

⑰ Fold tip toward center along crease C (made in step 13).

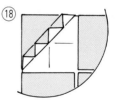

⑱ Origami should look like this. Repeat with remaining three sections.

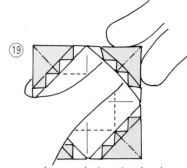

⑲ Open up each corner by inserting thumb as shown and at the same time pinching outsides. Firm up creases around the four central squares (inside dotted lines) to form base of dish.

COASTER

Use a piece of paper with a width twice the diameter of the glass to make a coaster that fits perfectly. Paper with striking colors —like gold or silver—makes especially attractive coasters.

Makoto Yamaguchi

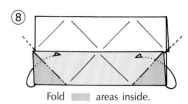

⑧ Fold ▨ areas inside.

①
Fold paper in half from top to bottom.

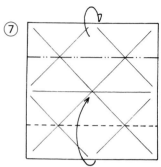

⑦ Fold bottom edge up to center line. Fold top edge under to center line.

②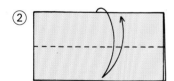
Fold in half again. Unfold.

⑥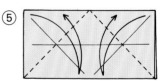
Unfold completely.

③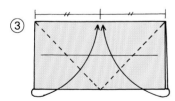
Fold both layers of lower corners up to top edge.

⑤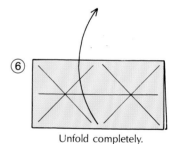
Follow steps 3 and 4 again, this time folding top corners down to lower edge. Unfold.

④
Crease firmly, then unfold.

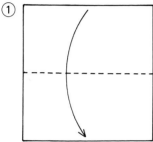

14

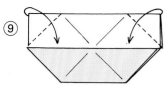

⑨ Fold top corners down to center line.

⑩ Fold in half, sliding top half into front of lower part formed in step 8.

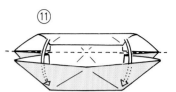

⑪ It should slide in like this.

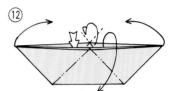

⑫

Gently push sides toward center to form square base.

⑭

Slip one coaster inside another to make a four-pronged coaster.

⑬ Finished coaster.

Origami games!

PARTY POPPER

The rule of thumb calls for a large rectangular piece of medium- or heavy-weight paper. A single sheet of newspaper (4 pages) folded in half will make a very loud popper!

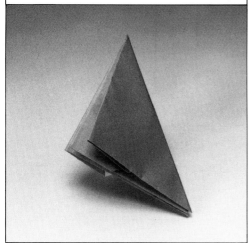

Traditional

①

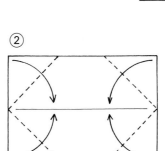

Fold in half. Unfold.

②

Fold corners in to center line.

③

Fold in half from left to right.

④

Fold in half from top to bottom.

⑤

Slide your fingers inside top flap, open, and flatten.

⑥

Fold bottom half of square up.

⑦

Repeat step 5 with bottom flap.

⑧

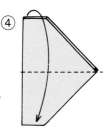

Fold three top triangles down.

⑨

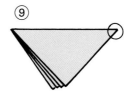

Hold corner of popper, then cock and snap your wrist. The inner flaps will fly open with a loud bang!

bang!

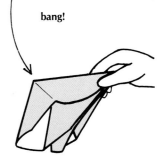

TOPSY TURVY

The Topsy Turvy will tumble well on any smooth, flat surface. A desktop or wood floor is ideal. Tap the Topsy Turvy gently if it does not tumble on its own.

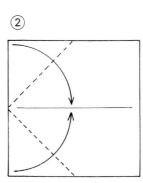

Seiryo Takekawa

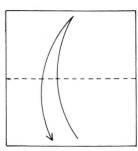

①

Fold in half. Unfold.

②

Fold corners down.

③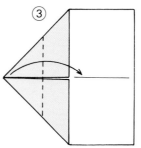

Fold corner in as shown.

④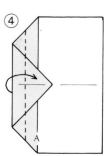

Fold edge in to line A.

⑤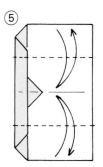

Fold top and bottom edges in to center line. Unfold.

⑥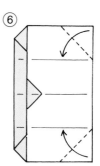

Fold right-hand corners down.

⑦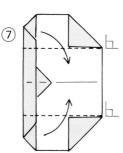

Fold top and bottom edges up. so that they stand upright at a 90° angle.

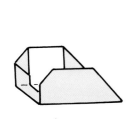

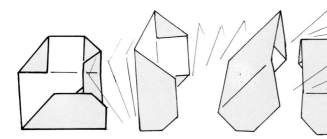

Stand the origami as shown. Release it and it will somersault.

PECKING CROW

Each time the crow pecks it hops forward. By tapping its tail continuously, it will race along. Mark off a finish line and race your crow against a friend's.

Traditional

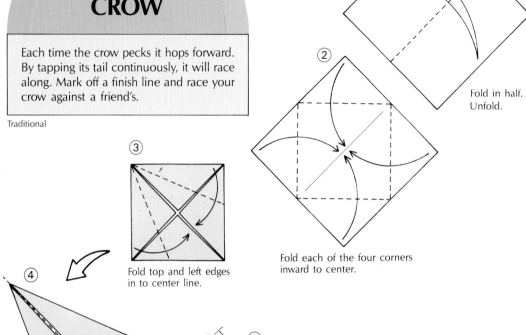

① Fold in half. Unfold.

② Fold each of the four corners inward to center.

③ Fold top and left edges in to center line.

④ Fold in half.

⑤ Fold █ area back along dotted line, unfold, then fold inward to form beak.

⑥ Draw eyes and wings.

Tap tail gently and crow will move forward with a pecking motion.

ROCKING PIGEON

If you cut off the corners in step 6 with a scissors and round off the bottom, the pigeon will rock even better.

Seiryo Takekawa

①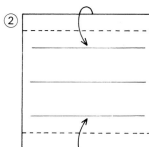

Fold in half, then unfold. Fold top and bottom edges in to center line, then unfold.

②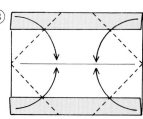

Fold top and bottom edges in as shown.

③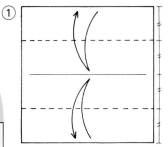

Fold each of the four corners in to center line.

④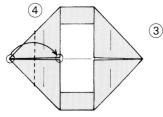

Fold left corner in, matching circled points.

⑤

Fold triangle back toward left.

⑥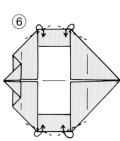

Fold four corners in just enough to make a rounded shape.

⑦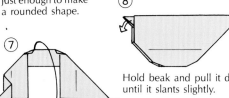

Fold in half.

⑧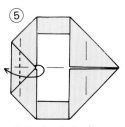

Hold beak and pull it down until it slants slightly.

⑨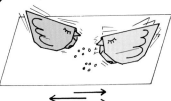

Draw eyes and wings.

Place pigeon on a piece of cardboard and move the cardboard sideways to make pigeon rock. Or tap tail end to produce a rocking motion.

ANIMAL FINGER PUPPETS

You can make five animal puppets with this same basic pattern. A small piece of paper (about 2″ x 2″) will make a decorative cap for a pen or pencil, and a large piece a hat (see facing page).

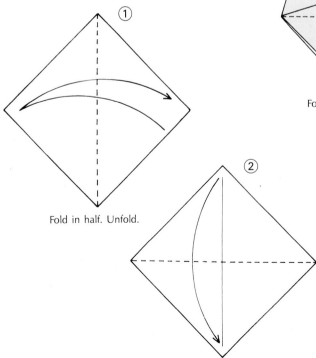

Traditional

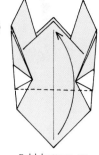

⑧

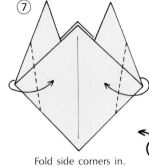

⑦

Fold side corners in.

Fold bottom up.

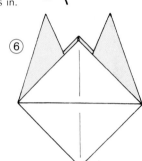

⑥

Origami should look like this. Turn over.

⑤

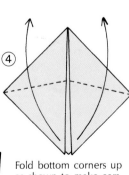

Fold top layer up.

④

Fold bottom corners up as shown to make ears.

① Fold in half. Unfold.

② Fold in half from top to bottom.

③

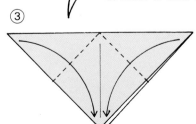

Fold top corners down.

⑨ Fold top corner forward.

⑩ Origami should look like this. Turn over.

⑪ This is the basic animal head.

⑫ Fold ears down for dog or pig.

⑬ Draw in face.

⑫ Draw in rabbit, fox, or cat face.

If you use a large piece of paper (as in the Samurai Helmet) you can make a hat.

CAWING CROW

With two crows you can have crow conversations with a friend. Or play Crows in a Row, a party game in which you pick up a small object in the beak and pass it to the next person as fast as you can.

Makoto Yamaguchi

① Fold paper in half. Unfold.

② Fold in half in opposite direction.

③ Fold two edges of triangle forward and align along center line.

④ Fold back two lower points as far as possible.

⑤ Pull inside layer out.

⑥ Origami should look like this.

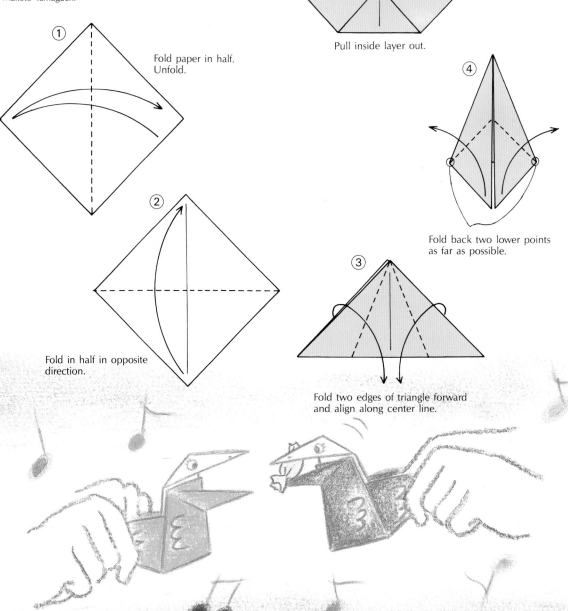

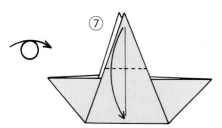

⑦

Turn over. Fold top layer down so that point meets bottom edge.

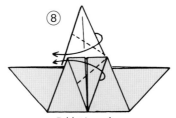

⑧

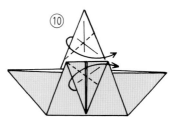

Fold triangular flaps to left.

⑨

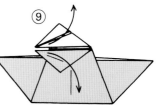

Unfold.

⑩

Fold flaps to right.

⑪

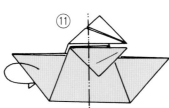

Fold in half.

⑫

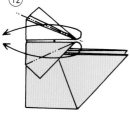

Pull top flap to left to form upper beak (using creases made in steps 8 and 10). Repeat with bottom flap.

⑬

Draw eyes and feathers.

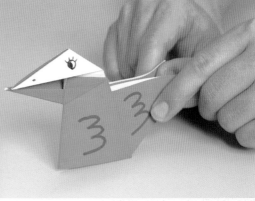

Open and close wings to make crow caw or "talk."

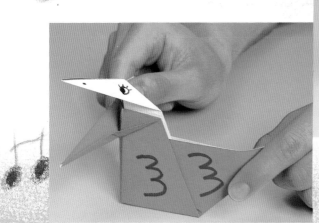

PLANE WITH COCKPIT

This plane is simple to make and flies straight and far. Be sure to test the "aero-dynamics" of the paper before you begin folding. Point the nose of the finished plane upward before "launching" it.

Makoto Yamaguchi

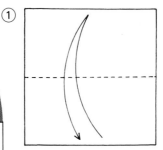

①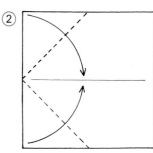

Fold in half. Unfold.

②

Fold corners down.

③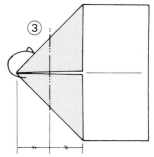

Fold corner under at halfway point.

④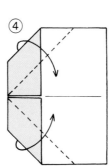

Fold clipped corners in, aligning extreme left edges at center line.

TESTING THE PAPER BEFORE FOLDING

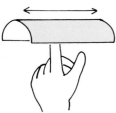

Balance the piece of paper on your fingertip. The sides that droop or curl under naturally will be the sides of the plane. The other two sides will be the front and back.

⑤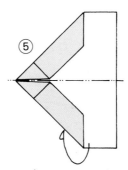

Fold bottom half under.

⑥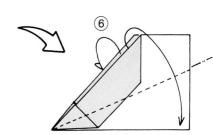

Fold top layer forward, aligning along bottom edge. Repeat on other side.

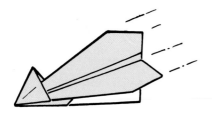

⑧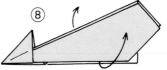

Bring wings up to horizontal position.

⑦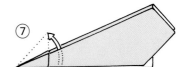

Pull out inner triangle and crease to form cockpit.

Flying origami!

JET PLANE

Any lightweight rectangular paper, such as notepaper, works well. As in Plane with Cockpit, point nose up.

Traditional

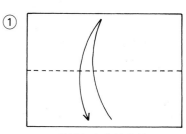

1

Fold in half. Unfold.

2

Fold corners down.

3

Fold triangle forward as shown.

4

Fold corners down.

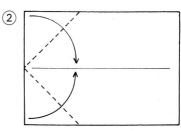

9

View from back. For plane to fly well, wings should be perfectly horizontal.

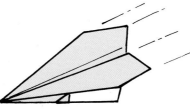

8

Bring wings up to horizontal position.

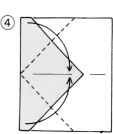

5

Fold small triangle to the left.

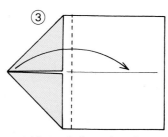

6

Fold bottom half back.

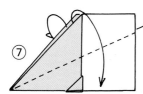

7

Fold front layer forward, aligning along bottom edge. Repeat on other side.

FLAPPING DOVE

The wings flap so realistically it seems as if it might fly away. Use a lightweight paper for a better effect.

Makoto Yamaguchi

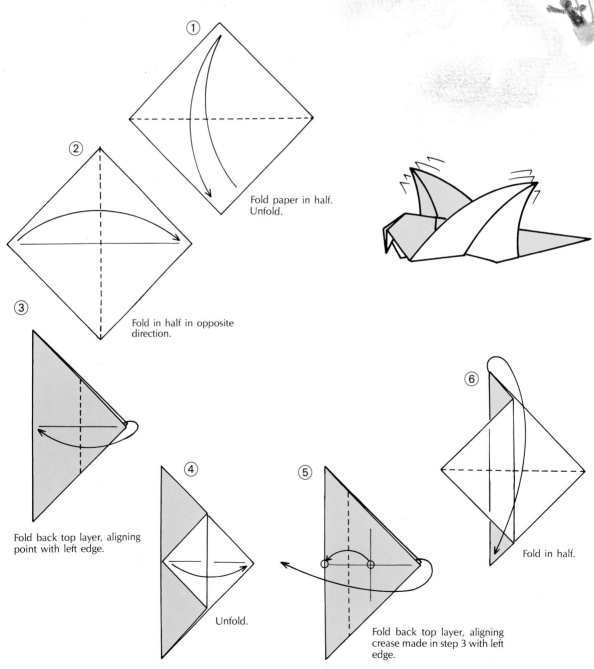

① Fold paper in half. Unfold.

② Fold in half in opposite direction.

③ Fold back top layer, aligning point with left edge.

④ Unfold.

⑤ Fold back top layer, aligning crease made in step 3 with left edge.

⑥ Fold in half.

Hold head and tail and pull
gently to make wings flap.

⑫

Fold ▨ area inward to form head.

⑪

Fold flaps under to form tail.

⑩

Repeat on other side.

⑨

A

B

Insert finger and pull down
to form folds A and B.

⑦

⑧

Fold top layer up, matching
circled points.

Repeat on other side.

27

RISING MT. FUJI

This fascinating trick relies on the friction of the paper to make Mt. Fuji rise from within. It is also known as the Climbing Monkey.

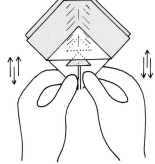

Origin unknown

①

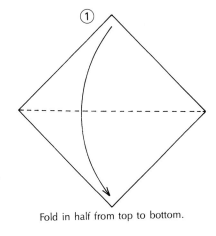

Fold in half from top to bottom.

②

Fold in half from right to left.

③

Open top triangle and flatten into a square.

④

Origami should look like this. Turn over.

⑤

Fold right flap to the left.

⑥

Repeat step 3 with left flap.

Hold points with thumbs and middle fingers and insert index fingers in folds. Move points up and down. The top will gradually rise.

⑦

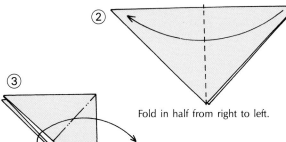

Fold bottom corner of top layer up. Turn over and repeat on other side.

⑧

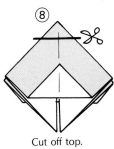

Cut off top.

⑨

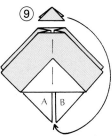

Thread points A and B through grooves of top.

FLAPPING CRANE

The crane is one of the best-loved motifs in Japan. Here is one of the more memorable origami cranes. Use light-weight paper for the best results.

Traditional

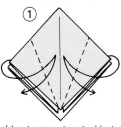

① Fold as in steps 1 to 6 of facing page, then fold both corners of top layer in to center line. Unfold.

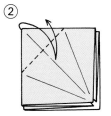

② Fold top corner down as shown. Unfold.

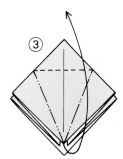

③ Bring bottom corner of top layer up, opening up as you do so. Fold sides in to center to form a diamond shape.

④ Origami should look like this. Turn over.

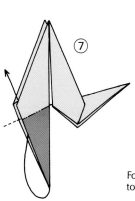

⑤ Repeat step 3.

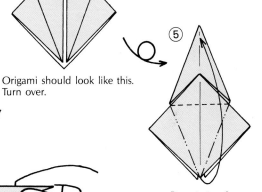

⑩ Bring wings up.

Hold crane as shown and pull to make wings flap.

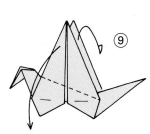

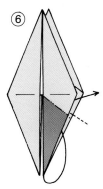

⑨ Fold wings down as shown.

⑧ Fold ▓ area inside to form beak.

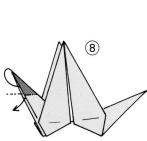

⑦ Fold ▓ area inside to form head.

⑥ Fold ▓ area inside as shown to form tail.

JUMPING FROG

Jumping contests are a natural here. See which frog can leap the farthest or the highest, or have an out and out race. They say that if your frog lands on its back on the first jump, it will rain tomorrow!

Traditional

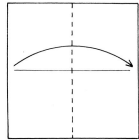

⑦

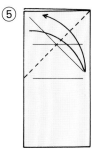

Fold bottom edge up to lower edge of triangle.

⑥

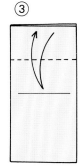

Using creases made in steps 3 through 5, fold top half inward to form triangle.

⑤

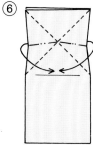

Fold left-hand corner down as in step 4. Unfold.

①

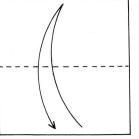

Fold in half. Unfold.

②

Fold in half from left to right.

③

Fold top half down to center line. Unfold. Turn over.

④

Fold top right-hand corner down to center line. Unfold.

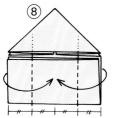

⑧ Fold sides of rectangle and back flap of triangle forward.

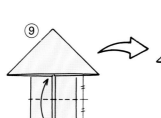

⑨ Fold bottom edge up to lower edge of triangle.

⑩ Fold top corners of rectangle down to bottom edge. Crease firmly.

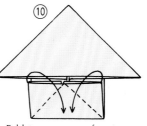

⑪ Pull [ ] triangle outward and flatten well.

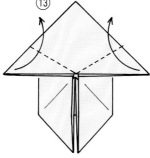

⑬ Fold outer corners of triangle up to form front legs.

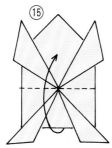

⑫ Bring outer corners forward and fold down.

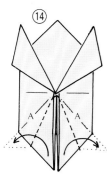

⑭ Fold bottom corners outward, aligning with lines A, to form back legs.

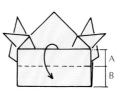

⑮ Fold bottom half up at point where four legs meet.

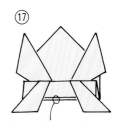

⑯ Fold down so that width of A is shorter than B.

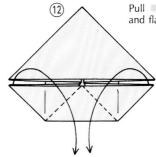

⑰ Bottom edge should protrude slightly. Turn over.

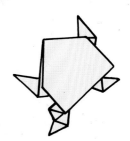

To make frog jump, press down back end of frog and draw your finger back.

MAGIC TRIANGLE

Place the Magic Triangle on a flat surface and release it gently. Wait a moment and the triangle will suddenly stand up of its own accord. The longer it takes, the more mysterious it is!

Seiryo Takekawa

①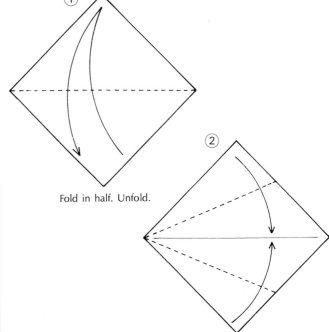

Fold in half. Unfold.

②

Fold top and bottom corners in to center line.

③

Fold right triangle under.

④

Fold corners in to center line.

⑤

Origami should look like this. Turn over.

⑥

Fold left corner forward as shown.

⑦

Origami should look like this. Turn over.

⑧

Fold corners in to center line.

⑨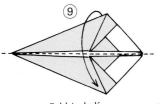

Fold in half.

boing!

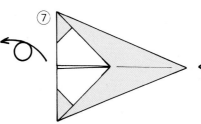

Place finished triangle on a smooth surface. Wait a moment…suddenly it pops up.

WHIRLY TWIRLY

Use patterned paper for an interesting effect. Instead of gluing the paper together in step 6, you can tape or staple the base after positioning the rotors in step 8.

Makoto Yamaguchi

①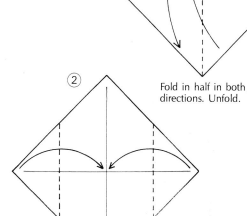

Fold in half in both directions. Unfold.

② Fold left and right corners in to center.

③ Fold left and right edges in to center line.

④ Fold left and right edges in once more to center line.

⑤ Origami should look like this. Turn over.

⑥ 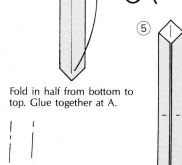 Fold in half from bottom to top. Glue together at A.

⑦ 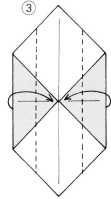 Fold tops down as shown to make rotors.

⑧ 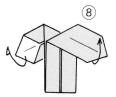 Bring rotors up until the surface of each is roughly parallel with floor.

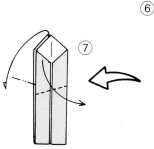 Throw Whirly Twirly high in the air, bottom end first. It will spin as it descends.

 For an interesting variation, insert a second Whirly Twirly into the first.

BARKING DOG

Place the paper colored-side up for the first fold. After making one or two dogs, use smaller sheets of paper to make puppies.

Paul Jackson

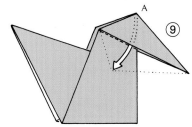

Pull out inside flap on each side, then flatten to form diamond shape.

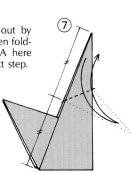

Turn ▨ area inside out by spreading open flaps, then folding them down. Point A here becomes point A in next step.

①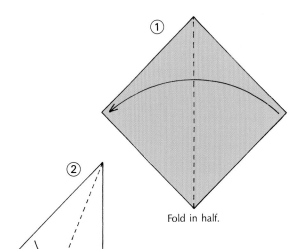

Fold in half.

②

Fold top layer to right, aligning with edge. Fold bottom layer under, aligning with right edge. Unfold both layers.

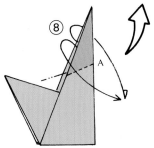

Fold top corner to the right as shown in diagram. Crease firmly. Unfold.

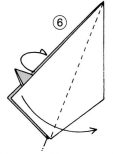

Fold top- and bottommost layers to the right along creases made in step 2.

③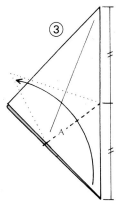

Bring bottom corner of triangle up and to the left, creasing at line A, as shown.

④

Unfold.

⑤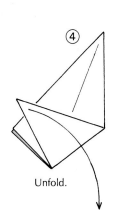

Fold ▨ area inside.

⑩ Fold to the left at A. Fold to the right at B.

⑪ Press to flatten creases made in previous step. Unfold.

⑫ Open head area from underneath.

⑬ Tuck in ▨ area.

⑭ Fold tip inside to form nose.

⑮ Pull nose down slightly.

⑯ Fold in at A. Fold out at B to form tail.

arf! arf!

Hold as shown. Pull hands in opposite directions and the dog will bark.

HANG GLIDER

Use origami paper colored on both sides to make a beautiful glider. Balance is extremely important, so fold exactly and use as little cellophane tape as possible.

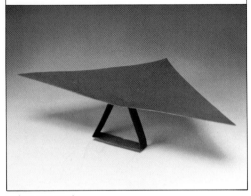

Makoto Yamaguchi

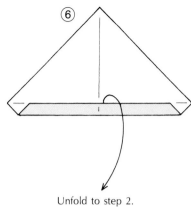

⑥

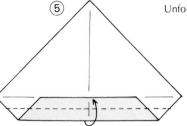

Unfold to step 2.

⑤

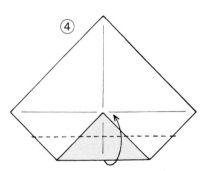

Fold bottom edge once more in to center line.

④

Fold bottom edge in to center line.

①

Place paper colored side up. Fold in half. Unfold. Turn over.

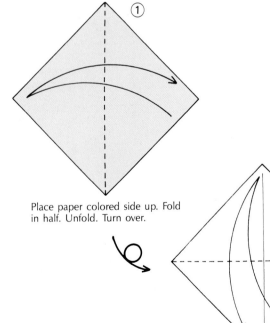

②

Fold in half from top to bottom. Unfold.

③

Fold bottom corner in to center.

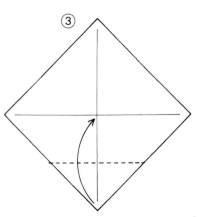

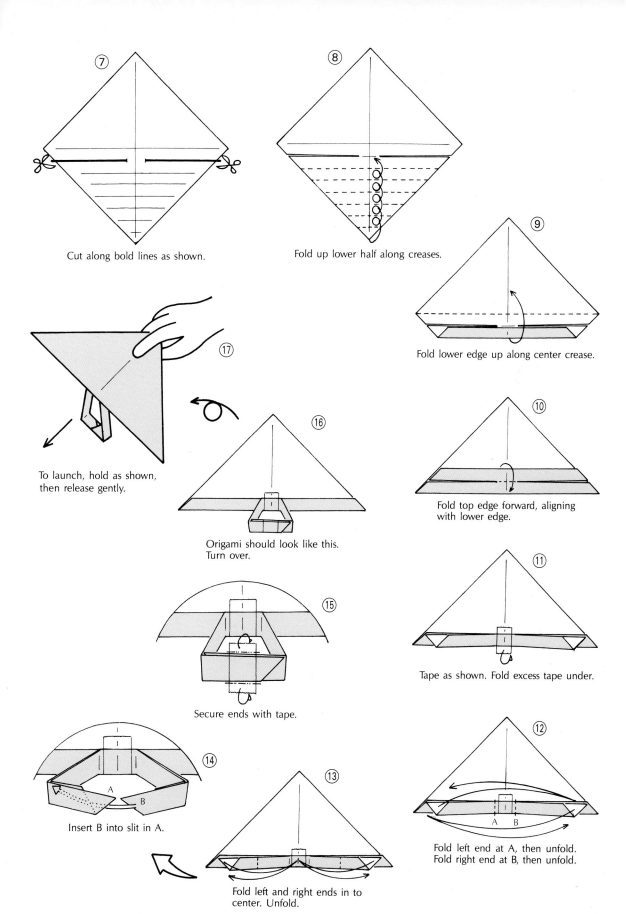

⑦ Cut along bold lines as shown.

⑧ Fold up lower half along creases.

⑨ Fold lower edge up along center crease.

⑩ Fold top edge forward, aligning with lower edge.

⑪ Tape as shown. Fold excess tape under.

⑫ Fold left end at A, then unfold.
Fold right end at B, then unfold.

⑬ Fold left and right ends in to center. Unfold.

⑭ Insert B into slit in A.

⑮ Secure ends with tape.

⑯ Origami should look like this. Turn over.

⑰ To launch, hold as shown, then release gently.

FOX FINGER PUPPET

Use brown or silver paper for a realistic-looking fox. A large fox puppet makes an excellent memo holder.

Traditional

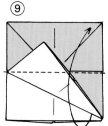

⑩ Fold bottom corner under.

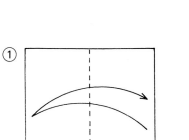
① Fold in half. Unfold.

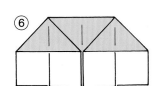
⑨ Fold front layer up again.

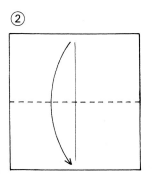

② Fold in half from top to bottom.

⑧ Fold bottom corner of front layer up.

⑦ Fold left and right sides in to center line.

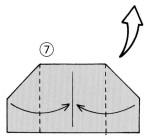

⑥ Origami should look like this. Turn over.

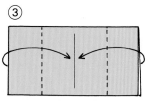
③ Fold left and right sides in to center line.

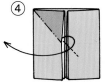
④ Pull out ▨ area and flatten to form triangle.

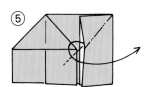
⑤ Repeat on right side.

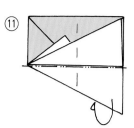

⑪ Fold remaining flap under.

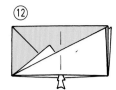

⑫ Slide your finger inside to open.

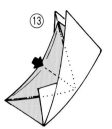

⑬ Push center point (black arrow) in to form mouth.

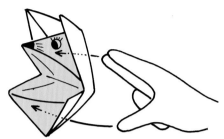

Insert fingers and thumb to open and close mouth.

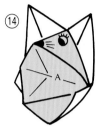

⑭ Crease line A firmly. Draw eyes and nose.

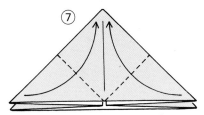
BALLOON

Bat this paper balloon back and forth using the palm of your hand. How long can you keep it in the air? For a "water balloon" (see facing page), heavy-weight or waterproof paper is better, but not a must.

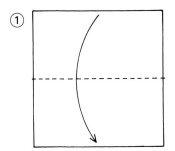

Traditional

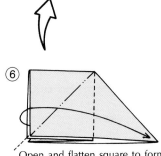

⑦ Fold left and right corners of top layer up.

⑥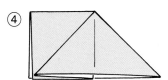

Open and flatten square to form triangle as in step 3.

⑤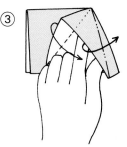

Fold right flap to the left.

④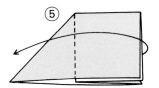

Origami should look like this. Turn over.

①

Fold paper in half from top to bottom.

③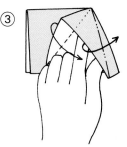

Slide your fingers inside top flap. Open and flatten to form triangle.

②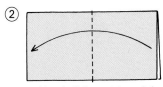

Fold in half from right to left.

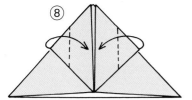

⑧ Fold left and right corners in to center line.

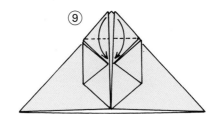

⑨ Fold top corners down.

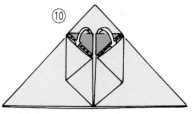

⑩ Slide ▨ areas completely into slots.

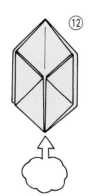

⑫ Inflate by blowing at bottom.

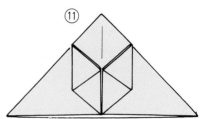

⑪ Origami should look like this. Turn over and repeat steps 7 through 10.

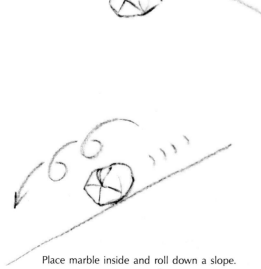

Place marble inside and roll down a slope.

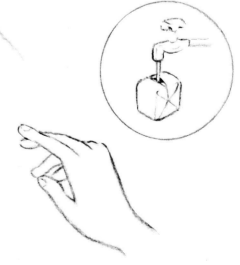

Depress one side of top to create gap. Tilt balloon and fill with water from the tap.

SUMO WRESTLER

Make several wrestlers and use an upside-down cardboard box for a ring. Each player taps the box with his finger to make the wrestlers move. The first wrestler to fall or touch the edge of the ring loses.

Traditional

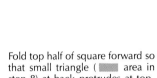

①

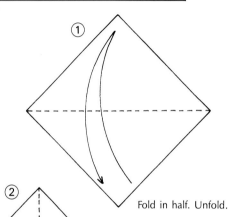

Fold in half. Unfold.

②

Fold in half. Unfold.

③

Fold each corner in to center.

④

Again, fold each corner in to center.

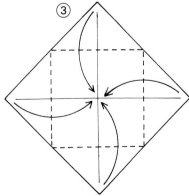

⑤

Origami should look like this. Turn over.

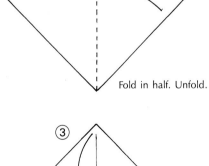

Fold left and right corners forward, without creasing triangular flaps underneath. Two triangular flaps will form a square at top.

⑥

Fold top half of square forward so that small triangle (▓ area in step 8) at back protrudes at top.

⑦

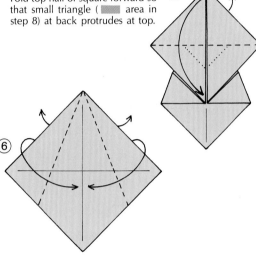

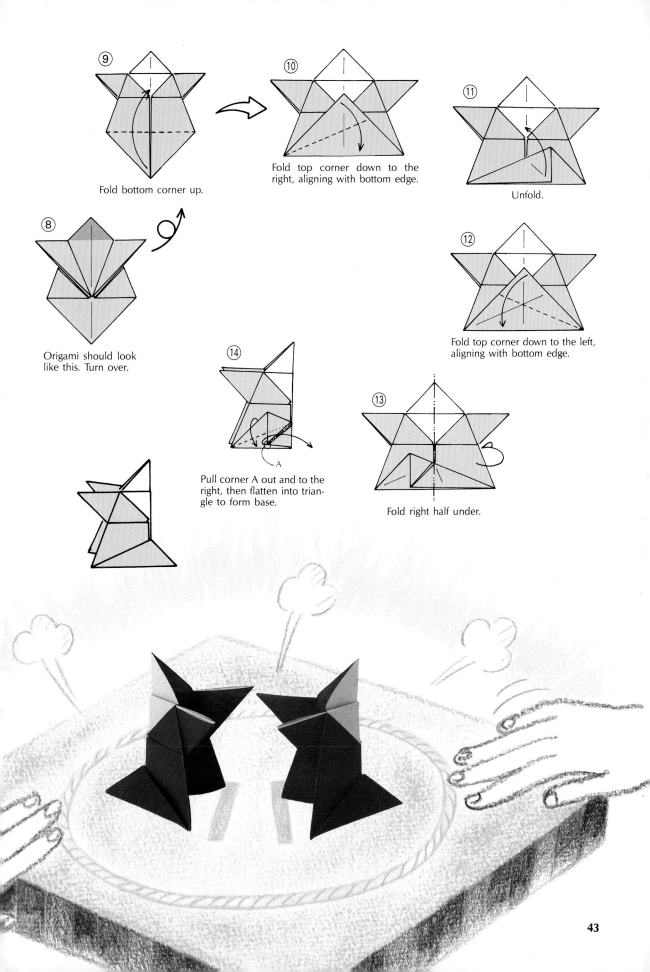

⑨ Fold bottom corner up.

⑩ Fold top corner down to the right, aligning with bottom edge.

⑪ Unfold.

⑧ Origami should look like this. Turn over.

⑫ Fold top corner down to the left, aligning with bottom edge.

⑭ Pull corner A out and to the right, then flatten into triangle to form base.

⑬ Fold right half under.

CAP

Use 2 large sheets of newspaper (8 pages) cut into a square (as in Samurai Helmet) to make this cap. It makes an excellent sun visor or baseball cap.

Makoto Yamaguchi

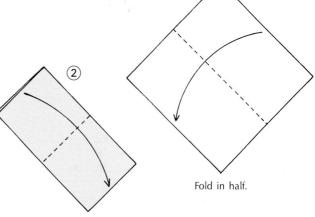

① Fold in half.

② Fold in half.

③ Fold in half.

④ Fold top three layers down.

⑤ Slide same three layers into pocket under top triangle.

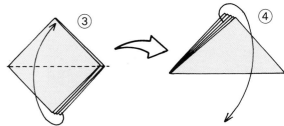

⑥ Fold top layer down as shown.

⑦ Unfold.

⑪ Fold corner of visor under. Fold side corners under.

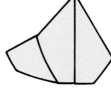

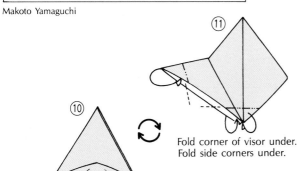

⑩ Origami should look like this. Turn sideways.

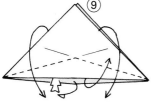

⑨ Pull down front flap and at same time open bottom.

⑧ Fold top layer down in other direction. Unfold.

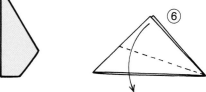

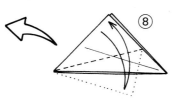

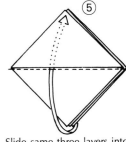

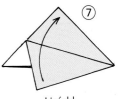

BASEBALL GLOVE

As with the cap on the facing page, use 2 large sheets of newspaper. This glove will catch and hold a ball firmly.

Makoto Yamaguchi

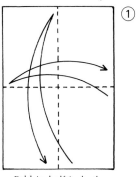

① Fold in half in both directions. Unfold.

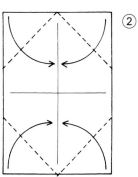

② Fold corners in as shown.

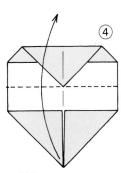

③ Fold top corner in to center.

④ Fold bottom half up along center crease.

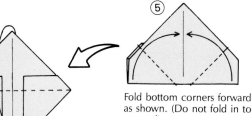

⑤ Fold bottom corners forward as shown. (Do not fold in to center line.)

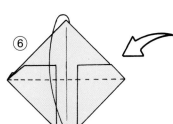

⑥ Fold top half down along center line.

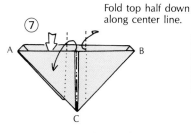

⑦ Bring corners A and B together, then rotate so that slit C is at bottom.

A   B

C

⑧ Origami should look like this.

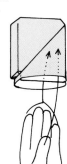

Insert your hand into bottom slots, pulling down slightly until balance feels right. Shape glove pocket with fist.

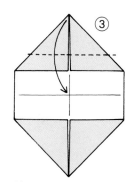

45

SAMURAI HELMET

Use newspaper to make a helmet that will fit, or use a small piece of colored paper for a doll's or toy soldier's helmet.

Traditional

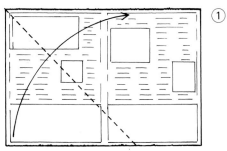

① Fold lower left corner up to top edge.

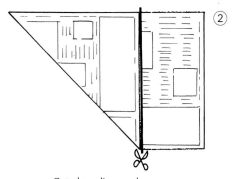

② Cut along line as shown.

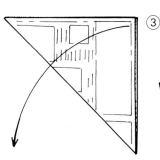

③ Unfold. Rotate so that crease runs from top to bottom.

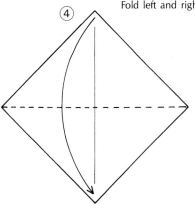

④ Fold in half.

⑤ Fold left and right corners down.

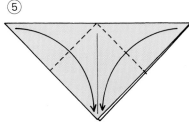

⑥ Fold top layer upward.

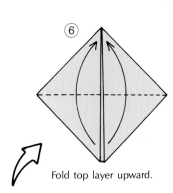

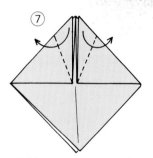

⑦

Fold top corners outward.

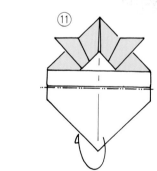

⑪

Fold bottom flap back.

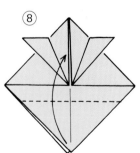

⑧

Fold bottom corner of top
layer up as shown.

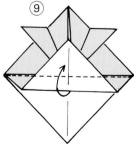

⑨

Fold lower edge of triangle
up along base.

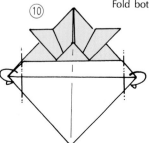

⑩

Fold left and right corners back.

Cleaning up!

ORIGAMI TOY BOX

Here's a box to keep all your origami in. Use a large, strong rectangular piece of paper about the size of a 4-page sheet of newspaper.

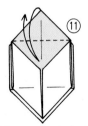

Makoto Yamaguchi

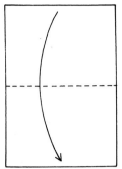

① Fold in half from top to bottom.

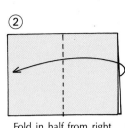

② Fold in half from right to left.

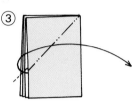

③ Open top flap and flatten into a triangle.

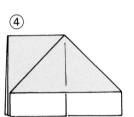

④ Origami should look like this. Turn over and repeat step 3 on other side.

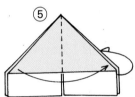

⑤ Fold front left flap to right. Fold back right flap to left.

⑥ Fold bottom corners of front layer up. Repeat on reverse side.

⑪ Fold top triangle in to center. Unfold. Turn origami upside down.

⑫ Pull triangular flaps to open and push bottom up at black arrow to form base.

⑩ Repeat steps 8 to 10 on reverse side.

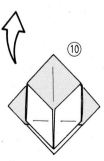

⑨ Fold ▒ area under, wrapping it around corners folded inside in previous step.

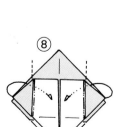

⑧ Fold left and right corners of top layer *inside*.

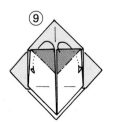

⑦ Fold left, right, and bottom corners of top layer in to center. Unfold.

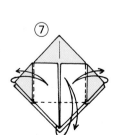